CW00404464

You are, aren't you?

poems by
MICHAEL ROSEN

Mushroom Bookshop, 10-12 Heathcote Street, Nottingham NG1 3AA.
Tel 0602 582506. *Jewish Socialist*, BM 3725, London WC1N 3XX.

Jointly published by Mushroom Bookshop and *Jewish Socialist*
Publications.

All rights reserved. No part of this publication may be reproduced,
stored in a retrieval system or transmitted in any form or by any
means, electronic, mechanical, photocopying, recording or otherwise,
without the prior permission of the author through the publishers.

ISBN 0 907123 09 0

Some of these poems first appeared in *When Did You Last Wash Your
Feet?* (André Deutsch, 1986), *Quick, Let's Get Out of Here* (André
Deutsch, 1983), *Mind the Gap* (Scholastic, 1992), *You Tell Me* (Kestrel,
1979), *Bloody Liars* (Michael Rosen, 1984), *Holocaust Denial* (Anti-Nazi
League, 1993), *Gulf War Poems* (East London NUT, 1992), *Give Me
Shelter* (Bodley Head, 1991), and *New Statesman & Society, Poetry Now*
and *Jewish Socialist*.

COVER PHOTO: Geraldine Clark Rosen
COVER DESIGN: David Rosenberg

Trade distribution through Central Books Ltd, 99 Wallis Road, London
E9 5LN. Tel 081-986 4854.

Printed in Great Britain by Aldgate Press, 84B Whitechapel High
Street, London E1 7QZ. Tel 071-247 3015.

Contents

Introduction

I was once asked to present the 'News Review' on London's daily Jewish radio station which is beamed out from a prefab behind Brent Cross Shopping Centre. (Brent Cross, a woman at the Radio Station told me, is so popular amongst the Jews of north London that a friend of hers asked that she should be buried there. She asked her why. 'So I can be sure that my relatives will come and see me.') On air, later, I happened to say that I knew I was Jewish because my parents told me I was and, though it might not suit everybody, that was all any Jew could go on. An enraged woman rang in to the station and said, 'Would you believe your father if he told you you were a dog?' I tried to explain that neither my father nor my mother did ever say that I was a dog... but I was stalling. I had lost the argument. Then it occurred to me that perhaps they did tell me I was a dog and all these years I've been lying to myself. Or maybe they told me I was a Jewish dog. Writing this book has brought to the surface some very important questions.

I haven't been asked back to Spectrum Jewish Radio but I think that was because I said that I didn't think Jerusalem was just a Jewish city. This didn't seem to me to be a particularly outrageous thing to say, but a woman rushed into the studio and handed me a piece of paper. I looked at it. It said: 'Please would you moderate your views.' I blanked out. Moderate my views? How do I do that? Are there places you can go to learn how to moderate views? I've got a lot to learn if I want a future in Jewish Radio.

Meanwhile, the Jewish Socialists' Group and Mushroom Bookshop asked me to assemble some pieces I had written that have a Jewish theme. I dug out the poems that were first published in *Jewish Socialist*. Then I turned to the ones that were first written for children's books and I found that I had quietly censored most of them, cutting out Yiddish words and expressions that I would normally have used: 'Grandfather' instead of *Zeyde'* and the like. Had I done this to make myself more acceptable? Probably.

By and large, my parents didn't make me feel that I ought to make efforts to be acceptable. I knew the one about the Jews who were waiting in line for the firing squad and one of them says, 'Please can I have a blindfold?' And his brother standing next to him says, 'Shh, don't make a fuss.' Though, now I come to think of it, I remember one occasion when I came to school with a *Daily Worker* badge on my school blazer. It was the day after the annual May Day march. Mr Baggs stopped me in the corridor and looked at it.

'Oh you're a Communist, are you?'

I went home and told my mother that Mr Baggs had asked me if I was a Communist.

'What did you say?'

'I said we were.'

'But look at your shoes,' she said, 'you haven't cleaned them for days.'

That's a Jewish Communist Mother Story. Glancing down at my shoes I notice that I still haven't cleaned them for days, so that bit of chiding didn't work. The Jewishness, we've cleared up, I'm a Jewish dog, but as for the Communism, that's another story.

I was ten in 1956 and I remember standing in Trafalgar Square and Nye Bevan is speaking from the plinth. Suddenly, one of my parents' Communist friends appears. His lips are tight and he says, 'They've done it, the tanks have gone in.' I'm thinking that this has something to do with the man who wears a hat named after him, Anthony Eden. But then I gather it has to do with a place called Budapest. The family connection with 'The Party' ended there, (which meant no more *Daily Worker* bazaars) but for me a long, meandering path began there, looking for socialist and marxist alternatives to the Soviet disaster.

As I write, something called an 'economic recovery' is supposed to be underway, which will mean, I gather, that millions of people will not be able to work, thousands of people will have nowhere to live, and there will be at least five places in the world where a war will be going on using weapons that I've helped to pay for. Meanwhile, anyone trying to get away from those wars will not be allowed to live here, I am told, in case it makes me racist.

I would like to thank Ross Bradshaw of Mushroom Bookshop and Julia Bard of *Jewish Socialist* for asking me to get this book together. I fought against the idea at first, thinking it would make me like the Jewish student who, some time earlier this century, was asked to write an essay on elephants. The American in the class wrote an essay called: The World's Biggest Elephant. The French student wrote one called: Elephants and Love. The English student wrote one called: Elephants and Big Game Hunting and the Jewish student wrote one called: Elephants and the Jewish Question. However, Ross and Julia persisted and thanks for that. I would like to thank my grand-

6

parents, my parents and my brother for looking after me, and asking me to save them the hole in the bagel. I would like to thank my wife and children for putting up with my telling them, over and over again, how my mother used to send me off to school with a new and horrible shirt with, 'It's good, have it. They're wearing them like that now.' And how when I came home she would always say, 'So? Did they like the shirt?' I would like to thank them for putting up with me standing at the door, when they come home, saying 'So? Did they like the shirt?'

Finally, just in case there is anyone out there bothered about whether what follows really is 'Poetry', can I say, don't worry. Just call it 'Bits' or 'Stuff'.

Michael Rosen
October 1993

Ice cream

At home,
when we had ice cream
we'd all sit round eating it
going
'Mmmm, this is nice. This is really nice.'
But then my dad'd say,
'You know what this could do with?
Just a little bit of fruit salad with it.'

So next time we had ice cream
we had ice cream
and
a little bit of fruit salad with it,
and we'd all sit round eating it
going,
'Mmmm, this is nice, this is really nice.'
But then my dad'd say,
'You know what this could do with?
Just a few chopped nuts on the top.
That would really make this perfect.'

So next time we had ice cream
we had ice cream, a little bit of fruit salad
and
a few chopped nuts over the top,
and we'd all be sitting round eating it
going
'Mmmmm, this is nice, this is really nice.'
But then my dad'd say,
'You know what this could do with?
A few of those
little tiny bits of chocolate
scattered over the top
that would make it — '

But my mum wouldn't let him say any more.
She goes,
'You're always the same, you are.
Nothing's good enough for you, is it?
I'll tell you something —
if you don't like this café
find another one.
You know why you're like this?
I'll tell you.
It was your *bubbe*.
She pampered you.
You were pampered, you were.
All I ever hear is,
'No one ever makes it like my *bubbe* did.'
Well, you can get this into your head:
I'M NOT YOUR *BUBBE*.'

And my dad'd turn to us and go
'What did I say?
What did I say wrong?'
All I said was,
'A few little bits of chocolate
scattered over the top
would be very nice.
What's wrong with saying that?
A few bits of chocolate
would be very nice, wouldn't they?
What's all the fuss about?
What
is
all
the
fuss
about?'

Bubbe and Zeyde

We sometimes see them on Sunday.
They live in a dark room at the end of a dark corridor
and *Bubbe* kisses us all when we arrive.
She looks like Mum but very silver and bent at the middle,
which we will all look like one day, says *Zeyde*.
Dad always looks fed up because he doesn't want to come
but Mum talks to them properly
Zeyde looks tired from working in the cap factory
and pretends that the half-crown he's going to give me
disappears into the ceiling along with my nose
if I'm not careful — snap — and there's his thumb in his fist,
and he beats me at draughts, dominoes, snap, hare-and-hounds
and even dice
and he's got a bottle with a boat in it
and we go for walks on Hackney Downs
which he calls Acknee Dans.
And all the old men there say,
'Hallo Frank,'
and while we're walking along he says,
'What's to become of us, Mickie, what's to become of us?'
and I don't know what to answer.
And he shows me to Uncle Hymie
who looks out of his window and says,
'Is that big boy your grandson, Frank?'
(even though he knows my name)
because that's the way they talk.
And when we get back
we eat chopped herring or chopped liver
which is my favourite
and *Bubbe* tells stories that go on for hours
about people she knows who are ill
or people who've had to pay too much money
and at the end of the story
it always seems as if she's been cheated.
And once she took a whole afternoon to tell Mum
how to make pickled cucumber and she kept saying,
'Just add a little salt to taste, a little salt to taste,
just taste it and see if there's enough salt,

to make sure if there's enough salt — just taste it and see.'
And she says to me, '*Tottelle*, come to *Bubbe*,'
and rubs my hair and bites her lips
as though I'm going to run away
and so she shakes her head and says,
'Oy yoy yoy yoy yoy.'
But *Zeyde* goes to sleep in the old brown armchair
with his hands in the pockets of his flappy blue trousers
and when we go, Mum frowns
and *Zeyde* holds my hand in his puffy old hand,
keeps ducking his head in little jerks
and says to us all, come again soon,
but I'd be afraid to go all the way on my own
and it's very dark and the lavatory is outside
which is sometimes cold.
Bubbe doesn't like it when we go
and she kisses us all over again
and Dad walks up and down like he does at the station
and Mum keeps pushing me and poking me
and they both wave all the time we go away into the distance
and I always wave back because I think they like it
but Mum and Dad sit absolutely quiet
and nobody speaks for ages.
Mum says *Zeyde* shouldn't give me the money.

Newcomers

My father came to England
from another country
My father's mother came to England
from another country
but my father's father
stayed behind.

So my dad had no dad here
and I never saw him at all.

One day in spring
some things arrived:
a few old papers,
a few old photos
and — yes —
a hulky bulky thick checked jacket
that belonged to the man
I would have called 'Grandad'
The Man Who Stayed Behind.

But I kept that jacket
and I wore it
and I wore it
and I wore it
till it wore right through
at the back.

Easter

At Easter things got pretty serious at our school.
Before the event there was an enormous amount
of hymn practice and when we sang:
'There is a green hill far away
Without a city wall...'
every year they told us
that it doesn't mean
that the green hill hasn't got a city wall.

Then we went back to class and they told us the story:
those horrible Jews getting him
and poor old Pontius Pilate not knowing what to do
and then hammering nails through his hands and feet
then afterwards with him wandering down the street
and Thomas sticking his fingers
into this bleeding hole in his side...
the whole thing was pretty serious and pretty messy.

I felt a bit bad about those Jews.
I mean I didn't think *Zeyde*'d do a thing like that
and I kept my head down in class
in case anyone thought I was in on it too.
But as Jesus was a Jew as well
I didn't see why I should get it in the neck.

As for Pontius Pilate, I found out later
he was really like any other ordinary Roman psychopath
and loved stringing people up
especially Jews.
Strange story —
a bit too violent for kids, I should think.

Zeyde

When we go over to *Zeyde*'s
he falls asleep.

When he falls asleep
he snores.
When he wakes up
he says
did I snore?
did I snore?
and we say,
no, of course you didn't.

The wedding

Uncle Ronnie got married in *shul*
my dad was the best man
there they all were standing under the *khuppe*
and the Rabbi is talking
and *Bubbe* is watching from her wheelchair
and it's time for my dad to hand Ronnie the ring.

Out it comes and just as my dad gives it to him
Ronnie faints.
Out cold.
Bubbe starts crying,
and everyone in the *shul* starts talking and tutting.
So Eileen's brother got his shoulder in tight on Ronnie
on one side
and my dad got his shoulder in tight on Ronnie
on the other
and the *shammes* propped him up from behind
and that was Ronnie's wedding.

Bubbe said later it was a terrible shame
he missed it.

Gypsy

My mother looked in the mirror
and said, there's gypsy in me.
She pulled a red scarf
tight over her head
and tied it at the back of her neck.
How could she be a gypsy? we said.

When Uncle Ronnie got married
an old woman who I'd never seen before
sat next to *Bubbe*.
She had gold earrings and a gold tooth
her skin was dark
she laughed at the food
and pointed at me saying:
who's this? somebody tell me who this is?

who's she? I asked later.
Bubbe's sister.
I never saw her again.
She was wearing a scarf
tight over her head
tied at the back.

Maths

We were sitting in Maths
Room eleven
sun streaming in through the windows
blackboard covered in hundreds of tiny numbers.
(If he wrote his numbers bigger
there'd be a chance you could understand
some of it)

The door opens.
It's the secretary
with a new bloke.
He's going to be in our class.

Stare stare whisper whisper.

Sandra Wilson and Diane Rose look at him.
It looks like they think he's amazing.
Really nice.
Diane Rose is Jewish and Sandra Wilson wishes she was.
Diane Rose only goes out with Jewish fellers.
Well,
she can only take someone home
if he's Jewish
otherwise she'll get it in the neck
from her dad.
Her mum as well, actually.

So she says, if she fancies a non-Jewish boy
she keeps it to herself
and tries to forget about him.

Anyway,
mostly she goes to Jewish clubs
so it doesn't often crop up.

Except in school.

And Diane Rose says she can tell
if someone's Jewish.
So the new feller walks in
right in the middle of maths.

Sandra Wilson and Diane Rose
are pretty excited about it.
Sandra Wilson opens her eyes up
and she starts to speak
without making a sound,
across the room
to Diane Rose.

'Jew-ish?' mouthes Sandra Wilson.
'Who? Him?' mouthes Diane Rose.
Sandra Wilson nods.
Diane Rose stares at him.

She looks back at Sandra Wilson.
'Ye-es. Ye-es.' Big nodding.
She's certain.

Maths teacher stands up.
'Right you can stop working.'
(It's alright, we hadn't started.)
'We've got a new boy
joining us from today.
His name is Sunil Gupta.'

Diane Rose looks at Sandra Wilson.
Sunil Gupta?
That's no Jewish name...
Sunil told us later

his old man was Indian
wanted him to do well in exams
so he wasn't going to muck about
or anything.

Later,
well – about three weeks later
Diane Rose and Sunil
started going out together.

This ought to prove something.

Shlump

Mum doesn't often shout at me
but when she's fed up with me
she goes in for great long speeches
and she doesn't hear anything you say

she says:
I'm tired of seeing you in those trousers
why don't you go to the men's shop in the High Street?
What's it called?
Harry Boothroyds?

No, Mum, one's called Harry Reed
and the other's called John Booth

...or you could go and see the little man
under the bridge
and he'd fit you up with a nice pair of trousers,
that Harry Boothroyd he has...

No, Mum
one's called Harry Reed
and the other's called John Booth

...he's got nice trousers
you look a complete *shlump* in those trousers
I'd give you the money
you could go to Harry Boothroyd's tomorrow...

No, Mum
one's called Harry Reed
and the other's called John Booth

...you could look smart
those trousers are a disgrace
I'm ashamed to see you wearing them
I'm sure the Stollar boy
doesn't wear trousers like that
doesn't he get his trousers at Harry Boothroyd's?

He gets his trousers at Harry Reed's or John Booth's,
Mum.

...so what's the matter with you?
Don't you want to look smart?
All this don't-care-what-I-look-like stuff
where do you get it from?
You don't see me going about looking untidy
— your father maybe —
but even he goes and gets himself
a couple of suits at Harry Boothroyds

No Mum
Harry Reed or John Booth's

...I'm giving you the money.
Here. Go now
and don't come back
until you've got yourself a pair of trousers
I can't bear looking at you another minute...

Which one shall I go to Mum?
Harry Reed or John Booth's?

How should I know? I haven't heard of either of them.

Conspiracy

In 1956, after 30 years
my parents decided they weren't Communists any more.
My friend Trio told us that
Hitler had said there was a World Jewish Communist
  Conspiracy.
Trio knew about Hitler and filled his exercise books
with pictures of concentration camp commandants.
He could click his heels and say 'Ja, mein Führer'.
Me and Cheeps, the *Daily Worker* reader,
wondered if we were part of
the World Jewish Communist Conspiracy
and Cheeps, who was an expert on this matter
— and hormones —
said that what Hitler actually said was that
there was a World Jewish Capitalist Bolshevik Homosexual
  Conspiracy.
Cheeps also said that he was sure
that he was growing mammary glands
(Cheeps, that is, not Hitler).
I took this to mean
that Cheeps was worried that
maybe he was a World Jewish Bolshevik Homosexual
but he said that there was no relationship whatsoever
between men growing mammary glands and homosexuality.

Lynne

There were only five possible blokes at school
for Lynne to go out with.
As a member of
the World Jewish Non-Bolshevik, Non-homosexual,
Hairdressers Conspiracy
she knew that she could only choose from
me, Cheeps, Stoll, Marshall and Serlin.
I think I was the third try.
When I turned up on the doorstep after our first night out,
her parents had over Uncle Harvey and the Brookstones.
The Brookstones were hairdressers too
and when I walked in
they were in the middle of a disaster with the perm mixture.
It had leaked all over the garage floor.
It was winter
and perm mixture does terrible things when it gets cold,
they said.
Lynne's dad said to me,
so are you going into business?
What business are you going into?
Uncle Harvey and the Brookstones all laughed and said,
who does Morris think he sounds like
asking Lynne's new young man a question like that?
Uncle Harvey said, You'd better mind your light fittings, Alice,
if he's coming round again
but Lynne's mother, Alice, said that
it was lovely to see a big feller in the house
seeing as they were all such *shnips*.
Then Morris said,
he hasn't answered my question,
what kind of business is he going into then?
I said I thought I wanted to go to university
and I liked acting
but maybe I would be a teacher.
It hung in the air above the bagels and cream cheese
like something unpleasantly English.
When I said I didn't go to *shul*
I might just as well have been a Catholic.
I had only tried to be Jewish twice.

24

Trying to be Jewish 1

When I was seven
David Kellner came up to me at school and said,
You are aren't you?
What?
No, you are, I know you are, you are aren't you?
I'm sorry, I don't know what you mean, I said.
My mum says you are and she knows,
she says she knows you are from your name.
What?
You're Jewish aren't you?
I think so, I said.
There you are then, David Kellner said...
well, my mum says you should come to the synagogue
and do Hebrew Classes.

So I went home and said,
Er David Kellner says I should go to synagogue
and do Hebrew Classes.
I see, mum said.

Hebrew classes were run by Mrs Kellner
but there wasn't a synagogue yet.
It was a corrugated iron methodist chapel
without any methodists in it.
Zeyde thought it was hysterical:
So Michael's going to *kheder*! Michael's going to *kheder*!
Zeyde didn't go to *shul* either,
he went to Hackney Downs instead
and stood around with a lot of old men in dark suits
with shiny bits on the *tukhes* of their *gatkes*.

At Hebrew classes Mrs Kellner who was very small
and had a huge and very wonderful bosom,
taught me the letters.
I could only remember two of them.
They both looked like the letter seven
but they each had a dot in a different place.
One of them had the dot over the top

and the other one had the dot in the middle.
How do you tell the difference, said Mrs Kellner?
I'll tell you.
(I never told David Kellner
that I loved his mother's wonderful bosom.)
What happens, she said
when you get hit by a football over your head?
You say OH!
And what happens
if you get hit by a football in your belly,
you say OOOH!
There you are
that's how you tell the difference.
One says OH! And the other says OOOH!

This, I remember
but I left Hebrew classes
after they shouted at me on the outing to Chessington Zoo.
You don't have to learn Hebrew
from people who give you *tsurres* at Chessington Zoo.

Trying to be Jewish 2

The second time I tried being Jewish
was when Mr Adams the maths teacher came out.
None of the experts on Jewishness had spotted him
but he announced that he would run a Jewish assembly
and Marshall, Serlin and Stoll went straightaway.
Cheeps gave it a miss on ideological grounds
and I joined him.
They didn't run assemblies for Jewish communists.
I'd heard about the conscience clause
that said that schools have to lay on assemblies
but no one has to go to them.

I went to see the severely depressed deputy head.
I won't be going to assembly any more, I said.
Is this so that you can come to school even later than usual? he
said.
No it's because I'm an atheist.
There is another assembly, he said.
I know, I said. But I'm not going to *any* assembly.
Yes, I heard you say that, he said
but there is *another* assembly, you know.
Yes, I know, I said, I heard you say that
but I'm an atheist.
He wasn't impressed
but said that I would have to bring a letter from home.

I told my father
that I wasn't going to go into assemblies any more.
He said, is this so that you can go to school even later than
usual?
I said it was because I was an atheist
and so was he
and so was mum
so it was fair enough.
He said, *kvatsh!*
he didn't believe a word of it,
but he wrote the letter and I got out of assemblies.
I had stood up for atheism.

Then I became wild about Lynne.
There was only one thing for it.
Jewish assemblies.
I went back to the severely depressed deputy head.
I would like to go to Jewish assemblies, I said.
I thought you did, he said.
That's a much better idea.

So every day,
I sat with Stoll, Marshall, and Serlin
and we said the *Shemah*
and I tried to get as near as possible to Lynne.
but she always sat next to Rebecca Feinstein
who it was rumoured had been having it off
since she was thirteen
(was this possible?)
The breakthrough came just before Jesus Christ's birthday
when a whole mob of us
took part in that traditional Jewish custom,
carol-singing.
Sometime between We Three Kings and
Oh Little Town of Bethlehem
me and Lynne swapped jumpers.

Honan

When Mr Honan my Latin teacher
(who had said to me in the corridor
'We should have been
on the side of the Germans
in the last war.')
was leaving,
he said,
'Don't get rubbed out Rosen.'
And I thought of the corridor
and reckoned
if we had've been
I would've been.

New school

When I went to the new school
people noticed I was a Jew.

I was the only one.

So they did the jokes:
you know,

throwing a penny on the floor
to see if I'd pick it up

rubbing their noses

going 'my boy' and 'my life'
while they were talking to me.

And if ever I had to borrow any money
there'd be uproar
cheering, jeering,
'Don't lend him any money, you'll never get it back.'

Sometimes I'd go along with it
and I'd put on what I thought was
a Jewish voice
and say things like
'Nice bit of *shmatte*.'

It's like I was bringing *Zeyde*
into the playground
running round him going,
'You're a Jew. You're a Jew.'

It's like I was saying,
'Yes I'm a Jew
but I'm not like other Jews,
I'm an OK-Jew.'

But I wasn't.
For them I was just
Jew.

I was the Jew that it was
OK-to-say-all-the-foul-things-
you-want-to-say-about-Jews-to.

And I played along with it,
I thought it'd stop them hating me
but all it did
was make it easier for them
to hate all Jews.

Jewish Chronicle

I wrote a play and
the Jewish Chronicle rang my dad and said:
What *shul* do you go to?
My dad said, I don't.
And the man said, That's alright, we don't mind.
And my dad said, Is there any reason why you should?

Don't tell your mother

When my mum went to evening classes
my dad would say,
don't tell your mother — let's have *matzo bray*
she always says I mustn't give you that greasy stuff
she says it's bad for you.

So he broke up the matzos
soaked them in water
beat up an egg
dunked the matzos in the egg
and then fried them.

'They taste best fried in *hinner shmaltz*
skimmed off chicken soup,' he says,
'but butter'll do.'

It tasted brilliant anyway
we loved it.
Then we washed everything up,
absolutely everything,
and we went to bed.

Next day
mum says to us,
What did your father cook you last night?

Silence.

What did your father cook you last night?

Oh, you know... stuff...
...egg on toast, I think.

The job

After a long interview
Rosen was asked to see a man
with garters on his shirt sleeves
who kept opening and shutting a filing cabinet
and saying, We cherish our rebels.
Then he said, We'll go nap, now scoot.

Rosen discovered
that this meant he had been given the job.

Rosen met Roger in Staff Training every three months.
Roger told Rosen that he was doing very well.

Roger told Rosen that though he was doing very well
there didn't seem to be quite so many openings.

Rosen told Roger that some people in other departments
were keen he should work there.

Roger told Rosen that it looked interesting
but Rosen wouldn't like it.

Roger told Rosen to apply for Staff jobs.
Rosen heard he had got one of these.

Roger told Rosen that sadly, this was not the case.
Roger sent Rosen home on full pay.

Roger rang Rosen up once a week to say everyone
was doing what they could.

After several months
Roger told Rosen he had to meet Head of Staff Training.

HST said he was very glad to have had Rosen on board
but thought that it would be better if Rosen went freelance.

It took Rosen the time it takes
to walk from Broadcasting House to Oxford Circus
to realise he had been sacked.

Twelve years later Rosen opened the paper
and read that MI5 had thought it unwise
that Rosen be given a job.
Rosen thought about
Roger's kind honest face
Rosen speculated about:
Roger's brain, Roger's promotion prospects, Roger's mortgage.

Vietnam

I was in the middle of the Vietnam war
(Grosvenor Square — picked up, not charged
— all they had on the charge sheet was 'BIG')
when the trains stopped working,
standing on Marylebone Station
this American says:
You gotta bad back?
I have, I said.
Me too, he said.
Uh huh.
No trains, he said.
Looks like it, I said.
I'm going to Beaconsfield, he said, how about you?
Me too, I said.
I'll call my son-in-law, he said.

A few minutes later he said,
we take the Subway to Ruislip,
    he'll meet us.

On the Underground to Ruislip he said,
My name's Butcher, General Butcher.

David met us at Ruislip Station:
I have to look up a few things at the base, dad.
    That OK with you, Mike?

The gateman saluted the general
and we sat in the car park
David went to fetch his shirts
some big women in jeans stacked coke cans in their cars.

He saluted when we left,
we drove down the motorway

the general pointed at the fields:
      — you could get yourself a little farm here, David,
      settle down,
      raise a few hogs
      that kinda thing.

Aw dad.

School visit 1

I arrive at the school.
The headteacher says to me,
I'm so glad you could come
because you must understand
that the children here have no language.

That's funny, I say
I thought I heard quite a lot of noise in the playground.
They must have been saying something out there.

Ah well, no, not exactly no language, she says
bad language, not vulgar, mind –
anyway – you'll soon find out when you get in there.

130 seven and eight year olds come in
and we get along fine.
We have plenty to talk about
One boy tells me
he keeps his old Spiderman T-shirt tucked under the mattress
on his bed
so his mum can't get at it and use it as a duster.

I do
'Down behind the dustbin
I met a dog called Jim
He didn't know me
and I didn't know him.'
And one boy called out,
How did you know his name was Jim, then?

That had me beat.

Anyway, they leave,
and as I am leaving
the headteacher thanks me for coming to her school
and then explains to me, like many others before her,
that this school has children
who aren't a patch on the children in the school up the road.

School visit 2

The name tag on her pinny says, Patricia Kaufpisch.
I'm going to ask her if she knows what it means...
her father must have told her...
no, her father didn't tell her...
no, I can't tell her in front of her friends...
I've got to say why they called her Kaufpisch...
maybe I will tell her that old German joke...

There were these Jews, right?
living in Germany about 200 years ago, right?
and they were called ben This and ben That
so these Germans said to the Jews
if you want to be citizens of Germany
you've got to have German names, right?
but it'll cost you...
and if you haven't got much money
(money, Jews, geddit?)
you'll have to buy ones like
Ochsenschwanz, Eselkopf, Saumagen and Hinkedigger:
Oxprick, Asshead, Pigbelly and Cripple.
So this Jew comes up to the German in charge of names
and he says, I've come to buy a name for myself
have you got any of those pretty ones?
Rosenthal, Valley of the Roses, that sort of thing?
Sure, says the man in charge,
but Valley of the Roses doesn't come cheap
what sort of money are we talking about here?
Oh I've hardly got two coins to rub together,
says the Jew.
So what do you do for living, son?
says the man in charge of names.
I sell things, a bit of this, a bit of that.
Fair enough, says the man in charge, fair enough.
How's this for size? Kaufpisch. Sellpiss.

...if I could talk to her on her own, I could tell her
but she's saying, goodbye, thank you for talking to us,
Mr Rosen.
Rosen? It means roses.
So?
I was one of the lucky ones.

Jewish Museum

In the Jewish Museum in Melbourne
they showed a video:
The History of the Jews in Australia.
Very interesting.
I didn't know that on the very first fleet of convicts
that went out in 1788
there were eight or nine Jews on board.
One of them was Esther Abrahams
who had nicked some lace.

A couple of days later
I read that one of the first bushrangers
was a cattle-thief called
Teddy the Jew-boy.
He was hanged.

So there I was watching the video
and it got into
big Jews
great Jews
mighty Jews
governors, judges, generals...
...I should be proud
that a man who sent soldiers over the top
in the Great War (to end all wars)
was Jewish?

And on it went:
contribution to Australian violin playing
short story writing,
retail clothes selling
one of our boys did it
one of our boys did it
one of our boys did it.

Then suddenly
all change
and we weren't hearing about Australia anymore,
it was Israel.
There was:
The Beautiful Life on a Kibbutz.
There was:
Dangerous Left-wing Enemies of Israel.
And finally
in a great burst of Jewish Australian patriotism:
there was:
Jewish Australians
send more money per Jew
to Israel
than any other Jews in the whole wide world.
Music.
Credits.
Lights up.

And we looked at each other
feeling so pleased about that contribution
to armed terror in the Occupied Territories
and so nice and safe and welcome here in Australia
away from those police cells
where Aboriginals happen to die.

Duckslager

In the brochure it said,
modern bungalow on farm in picturesque scenery
ideal for North York Moors and coast.

when we got there
the bungalow was OK
but next to the orchard
there was barbed wire everywhere
high concrete walls
and there were 20,000 ducks
in a shed with no windows

Dave Rosenberg said:
'...and we never knew it was there...'

Cousin Ted

I went to see my father's cousin, Ted
in America
he told me about his uncle Morris
my father's father,
the one who stayed in America
when my father's mother came to England
with Sylvia, my dad and the baby.

Morris, he said, lived out of a metal trunk
with eight grey suits in it
and he did a lot of living,
I mean a lot of living.

He was union organiser for the boot and shoe workers
and travelled up and down the east coast
blackballed in factory after factory
stood for Senator
as a candidate for the Socialist Party of America,
in Pennsylvania in 1928
and always said he got more votes than his leader,
Norman Thomas who was running for President.

He always dressed immaculately, said Ted
he wore spats, straw hat and carried a cane.
When Morris got up to speak
people listened.

He never intended to follow the family to England,
Ted said.
A few days later
he told me that Morris stayed with a landlady for quite a time
and a few days after that
Ted said that once Morris had turned up
and had taken him on one side
put his hand in his pocket
and taken out a wallet.
Out of the wallet he took a picture of a boy
about nine years old.

What do you think of him? Morris said to Ted
He's a smart boy, isn't he?
He's going to do great things.

Back in England
my father and I were over at Sylvia's
and they were talking about the stuff
that was sent over from America when their father died.
He left some money to a landlady
who had been very nice to him, said Sylvia.

So I told them the story of their father and the photo of the boy.
Well, said Uncle Joe
she *was* very kind to him, wasn't she?

Two penn'orth of greens

My father said that his mother
used to send them out
to get two penn'orth of greens from the *hunk*
the woman on the corner of the street.
Shocking really to call her that, he said
it was because she had a hunchback.

A few months later,
Sylvia told me that their mother
used to send them out
to get two penn'orth of greens from the Hook
the woman on the corner of the street.
Shocking really to call her that, she said
it was because she had a hooked nose.

Leosia

I found my father's cousin
the one who had been put on a train in Poland
by his mother and father
said goodbye
went east and never saw them again,
the one who told the Russians
he didn't want to be a Russian citizen
so they sent him to Siberia;
the one who joined the Polish Free Army
when Russia joined the war
fought in Russia, the Middle East
North Africa, Sicily, Italy
and turned up on Aunty Sylvia's doorstep
at the end of the war saying,
Lady Sylvia? Lady Sylvia?

He's a taxi driver in Stanmore
but he wouldn't talk about any of this
but his wife told me about his Aunt Leosia,
who, when the Germans arrived
went west instead of east.
She put a crucifix round her neck
and took the diamonds out of her grandmother's brooch
and had them put into the heels of a shoe,
she thought she might be able to sell them
if she had any problems.

In Germany she worked in a munitions factory
no one ever found out she was Jewish,
she survived the war and went to Israel
to find her brother Naftali.

She told him how she had lived
with the diamonds in the heel of her shoe
and Naftali said, where did you get the diamonds from?
and Leosia said, from our grandmother's brooch.
So Naftali told her that many years before
their mother had written to tell him that

47

because of some financial difficulties
she replaced the diamonds on the brooch
with glass imitations
and sold the diamonds.
She hadn't told anyone of this but had written to Naftali
just to get it off her chest.

Leosia had gone through the war
with bits of glass in the heel of her shoe.

The promised land

So you live in Hackney? – why live in Hackney?
everyone moved out of Hackney
have you been to Israel? – my daughter lives in Israel
she married an Iraqi feller – Jewish of course
wife and I went out
we sold up here – sold the house the car – everything we sold
I was in computers here – writing programmes – doing very well
but over there – they wanted it all in Hebrew
I tried – I went to classes – the prayers I could read
but I was too slow – I couldn't work it on the computers
I couldn't get a job – they didn't want me
it got very hard – we couldn't talk to our grandchild even
he only spoke Hebrew – we spoke to him and he didn't
    understand
and we spent everything – we spent everything we had
all our savings, everything – we had nothing
so we had to come back
and here we had nothing – no house no car nothing

so now we're living in a little poky flat
you can see I'm too old to get a mortgage
and driving the taxi doesn't bring in enough
she's taken it very bad – she's ill
she's always got something wrong
she doesn't go to the toilet for a day – and it's bowel cancer
I'm not at home – I try to get her to go out
sometimes she does the catering at the synagogue
I showed my slides there last week – raised a few pound for
    aliyah
but only sixteen people came – they're good slides – Eilat,
    everywhere
and you know when we ring? – the little boy can't talk to us

that's £6.40 – nice talking to you – *zay mir gezint*

One of those

So where do you work, I said
At the solicitors in Mare Street, she said.
Which one? I said
Baxters, she said.
Oh, is he the Scots bloke, I said.
No, she said, he's one of those
and made a large semi-circle in front of her nose.
Oh yes, I said.
I'm one of those
and I made a large semi-circle in front of my nose.

Oh my God, she said
I had no idea
it's never occurred to me
all this time I've known you
and I never knew
I would never have guessed
oh I am so sorry
really I didn't mean any harm
I'm not prejudiced
really I am not
Oh my God
what have I said?

The Woolwich

Hallo Mr Rosen
said Mr Knight, the man at the Woolwich
how can I help you?

I said that I was wondering
if there was any way that I could raise some money
to pay for doing up the basement
and he said that building societies
were in the business of providing a competitive product
and I said that I was looking for a loan
not a product
and he said that's what he meant
but they were all in the marketplace now
so I said that was great
but could he or couldn't he give me some lolly
and he said that he could
and would I sign form 23/B
and for all he cared I could buy a speedboat with it,
and I said I didn't want a speedboat
I just wanted a new basement
and he said
that the satisfaction he got in life
was helping improve the quality of people's life
Thanks a lot I said.
Pleasure to do business with you, he said.
Goodbye, I said
Goodbye, Mr Cohen, he said.

Fighters for life

Our mothers and fathers
fought the thugs who came to torment them on the streets.
They organised in their places of work against magnates
who were pouring milk down mines, shooting miners
killing Afghans and hobnobbing with Hitler.

They fought the Nazi Axis
with the planes and tanks and machines

and millions wept.

Such a tale of separation of lovers, of brothers, of sisters,
of children, of husbands, fathers or mothers
such a fall of streets, towns, countries and continents
had never been known.

So much — so quickly
so much killing, plunder and ruin, so much energy, so much
power
so many brains, so many hands, making machines to break
machines.

Out of the blood and oil, out of the iron and steel
out of the fires and infernos, the burnt wastelands,
the pits and heaps of broken bones —
our mothers and fathers came together

and with them came the oil-owners, iron-owners, steel-owners
fire-owners, inferno-makers, waste-makers, home-breakers.

None of *them* had been in the sewers of Warsaw
they weren't on Main Street Hiroshima
they weren't eating rats in Leningrad
they didn't queue in the markets or at Auschwitz
they didn't set light to their own roofs
to stop enemies sheltering under them
they didn't stand at the benches and lathes
beg for water, wash pants, boil a potato, or pick apples.
They didn't even lift the gold they hoarded.

This gang of dictators, commanders, chiefs and bossmen
discuss how the power that lies in the earth of the Earth
shall be shared,
and commandeer the men, women and children
on the earth of the Earth to get it.

There is no trail of destruction of living things,
no trick, no system, no pain, no breaking of bodies
no sickness, paralysis or torment
no hunger, fear, fever or cold
that these men will ever hold back
from leaving in their path

who dies for them?
who died in Budapest? Haiphong harbour?
or on the streets of Derry?
who died in the football stadium of Santiago?
in the Sabra and Shatila camps?
or in Tiananmen Square?
who dies for Rio Tinto Zinc
the Chernobyl Nuclear Power Project
and the Grand Consolidated Gold Mine?

who gets maimed
making, building, washing, digging and cleaning?
who falls, who drops before their time?

People who have nothing
people who start every day with nothing
but their heads and bodies
people who hope to have strength enough
to work enough
to get food enough
to build up their strength enough
to work enough —

fighters for life.

Against this force of world work
a cellarful of worldwide chiefs and operators
rule and penetrate

every street corner, vineyard, barrack and mine
the fish-nets, stables and broom-cupboards,
the beaches, hospital bays and stoves.

Fighters for life, makers of life, lovers of life
we need ways of coming together and holding together
where we fight for life
where we make and love that life
or we will be called up for the armies of destruction
for the cellarful of worldwide operators
and so live to die.

Swear word

When little old women (as the books used to call them)
and little old men too, perhaps
ran little old corner shops
selling detergents and teddy bears, aspirins and oil
birthday cards and eggs
there was a special gleam in the eye,
a proud-to-be-British twinkle
aren't we cosy and quaint, safe and chatty,
sane little people at home with our corner shops?

But the big boys moved in:
Old WH Smith and his son, Big John Sainsbury
Big Boots the Chemist, King Tesco, Spar and Mothercare.
Big Fish eat Little Fish
and little old ladies' sons and daughters
became floor managers, office workers
salaried staffs and shop assistants
in developed town centres and shopping malls.

But now the aren't-we-cosy-and-quaint, safe and chatty,
sane little people snarl and spit about their corner shops.
The Great British love of high-price baked beans
at the corner shop,
doesn't make heroes out of little old Gujeratis
selling exactly the same detergents and teddy bears,
as ever was.

A new national swear word was born:
Paki-shop.

Sharansky

Remember Sharansky the freedom fighter?
A Jew in Russia
he said he was a refugee
in his own country.
Let me go to Israel, he said.
Let my people go.
He called out to the whole world
Has no one got the time to listen to us?
Will no one hear our cry for freedom?

In the end they let him go.

He arrived in Israel
and some people came up to him saying,
We are Palestinians
we are refugees in our own country
has no one got the time to listen to us?
Will no one hear our cry for freedom?

And Sharansky said,
Freedom? Freedom?
Sorry guys,
there isn't enough of that to go round for everyone.
Can't help you.

Enough

I've heard enough about Eichmann and Himmler
Heydrich and Bormann
– sadistic maniacs etc etc
I've heard anough about Hitler
– cunning diplomacy, magnetic oratory etc etc

Just tell me
who gave them the money to start the thing off.

Nazikraft

If all we had to do in life was
simply become more and more skilful
then we could admire and applaud
the craft and brilliance
of the engineers and fence-builders
the plumbers and welders
the fitters and designers
the draughtsmen and the architects
the planners and the chemists
who made Concentration Camps
the clever places they were.

Holocaust denial

Vultures cackled over our corpses:
their old dreams had taken shape:
we were carrion at last.

Vultures scoured and cleaned,
tidied up the carnage,
wanting no leftovers.

Vultures are looming now —
they hover over high-rise wrecks
and hungry queues,
hunting bodies,
screeching, 'Corpses? What corpses?
We're pretty boys!
Pretty boys!'

Parading as parrots,
they don't fool us —
because we are the leftovers,
the ones that poison vultures.

Let's play tyrants

take your map of the world
take your blue pencil
mark out the countries

help a coup over here
ignore a massacre down there
assassinate a leader over there

pick a colonel over there
pick a general round there
pick an air commander down here

lend them dollars
lend them sterling
lend them marks

sell them bombs
sell them tanks
sell them fighters

train their armies
train their airforces
train their secret police

send in Rio Tinto Zinc
send in Anglo-American
send in BP

get their bauxite cheap
get their tin cheap
get their oil cheap

watch the people starve
watch the people die young
watch the people get dangerous

watch the colonels fall out
watch the generals squabble
watch the air commanders fight

see the bombs drop
see the tanks roll
see the fighters fly

see the people die
see the villages burned
see the cities laid waste

sell more bombs
sell more tanks
sell more fighters

but oh dear your colonel gets out of control
      your general won't hand over the oil
      your air-marshal starts talking independence

now's the time to talk about freedom
now's the time to talk about democracy
now's the time to talk about standing up to tyrants

wheel out the B-52s
wheel out the cruise missiles
wheel out the lasers

and kill the people
kill them in their villages
kill them in their cities
kill them on their farms

so that they can have freedom
so that they can have democracy
so that they can be free of tyrants

Lessons to Arabs

oil in texas is texan oil
texan oil is not your oil
texan oil is our oil

oil in the north sea is north sea oil
north sea oil is not your oil
north sea oil is our oil

oil in kuwait is kuwaiti oil
kuwaiti oil is not your oil
kuwaiti oil is our oil.

our oil is not your oil
our oil is our oil
your oil is not your oil
your oil is our oil

The trouble with Saddam

trouble with Saddam Hussein, he's a military dictator
and we've never done business with military dictators
apart from Pinochet, Zia, Stroessner, Somoza, and Saddam
Hussein

trouble with Saddam Hussein, he's a ruthless fanatic
and we've never done business with ruthless fanatics
apart from Marcos, Shamir, King Fahd and Saddam Hussein

trouble with Saddam Hussein, he's a mass murderer
and we've never done business with mass murderers
apart from Pol Pot, Lyndon Johnson, George Bush and Saddam
Hussein

Places where...

...'the spectre of Vietnam has been buried at last' (Bush):

The White House
The Sun
Margaret Thatcher's head

Places where the spectre of Vietnam lives

Panama
Iraq
Vietnam

Twelve-years-of-Tory-rule-boogy

slump
war
boom
slump
war

Tory tongue-twister

The party of choice
chose to chop hospitals.
What choice hospital
for those whose hospital
was chosen for the chop?

(Say three times quickly.)

How many

for Mordecai Vanunu

how many people
who know,
don't say?

how many people
who say,
don't say it all?

how many people
who say it all,
don't get heard?

how many people
who get heard,
get rubbed out?

how many people
who get rubbed out,
get forgotten?

how many people
remember the ones
they want us to forget?

To suggest

Good evening

To suggest that huge empty office blocks
in Docklands
is in any way linked to the problem of the young homeless
is ridiculous

To suggest that the diminishing amount of council
  accommodation
through sales
is in any way linked to the problem of the young homeless
is absurd

To suggest that councils evicting squatters
from unused property
is in any way linked to the problem of the young homeless
is naïve

To suggest that landlords demanding evidence of a fixed address
before taking someone on
is in any way linked to the problem of the young homeless
is simplistic

To suggest that employers demanding evidence of a fixed
  address
before taking someone on
is in any way linked to the problem of the young homeless
is a misunderstanding

To suggest that difficulties in claiming benefit
and income support
is in any way linked to the problem of the young homeless
is just propaganda

To suggest that the property boom which pushed the cost of
  property
out of reach of the poor
is in any way linked to the problem of the young homeless
is preposterous

To suggest that
after many years of decline, Britain is now a land of opportunity
after many years of socialist stranglehold, we are now freer than
we've ever been
after many years of Welfare State nannying, young people on the
streets have got only themselves to blame
is much nearer the truth

thank you and goodnight,
(make it a double, George, I'm shattered)

English literature

George Macbeth, poet, now deceased
told his school readers
that T S Eliot's 'apparent antisemitism'
was not 'significant' or 'dishonourable'
as such references were 'frequent and casual'
in the writing of the time.

So, dear students,
do not concern yourselves with this matter,
the antisemitism of any writer
in the first half of the twentieth century
is here certified normal.

What fun it is to be a critic
reading poems that are antisemitic
Eliot, Chesterton, Thackeray too
loved to write of the hateful Jew
and good old Gilbert of Sullivan fame
pitched in against the hateful same.
Cuddly Stevie Smith as well
wanted us to go to hell.
Our lives are so much the richer
for reading English Literature.

I am a Jew

I am a Jew because my mother and father told me I was
I am a Jew because I don't believe in God
I am a Jew because I am told to be not so Jewish
I am a Jew because my mother told me about standing in Cable
Street in 1936 to stop Mosley from marching through
I am a Jew because my father told me that his grandfather told
   him that if you take one match you can break it, if you take
   two matches you can break them, if you take three matches
   even you can break them, but a whole box of matches you
   can't break — that's a Union
I am a Jew because you tell me that Jews are safe when I know
   that I am only as safe as the last Kaiser's tailor was
I am a Jew because I like the one about the Martians and the
   bagel bakery,
I am a Jew because I've never been to Israel
I am a Jew because I know there's no such thing as the Jewish
   race, the white race, the black race, the English race, my race or
   your race
I am a Jew because I saw two boys laughing at the Hasidim
I am a Jew because someone called me at three in the morning to
   tell me that I am a filthy fucking Jew
I am a Jew because I have gone ex-directory
I am a Jew because someone told me that he's not against Jews
   but there are too many Jews in high places
I am a Jew because I am looking forward to the time when there
   will be no high places

Glossary

Pronunciation
Kh sounds like the guttural ch as in lo*ch*
u is pronouced oo as in f*oo*t
ay sounds like the y in b*y*
ey sounds like ai as in d*ai*sy

Aliyah	emigration to Israel
bubbe	granny
gatkes	pants, trousers
hinner shmaltz	chicken fat
hunk	Who knows? See 'Two Penn'orth of Greens'
kheder	Hebrew classes
khuppe	canopy for wedding ceremonies
kvatsh	rubbish
matzo bray	see 'Don't Tell Your Mother'!
shammes	synagogue beadle
Shemah	the daily prayer
shlump	untidy, sloppy person
shmatte	cloth (literally, rag)
shnip	short person
shul	synagogue
tottelle	little daddy
tsurres	troubles
tukhes	bum
zay mir gezint	keep well
zeyde	grandad

mushroom
B·O·O·K·S·H·O·P

Mushroom Bookshop is Nottingham's independent bookshop,
run under workers' control since it was founded in 1972. Among
the shop's many specialisms are multicultural children's books
and books and music of Jewish interest.

To go on the free mailing list, write to 10-12 Heathcote Street,
Nottingham NG1 3AA. Tel 0602 582506.

Jewish Socialist

Jewish Socialist is a quarterly magazine dedicated to reaching the
parts of Jewish and socialist life that other publications do not or
will not touch. It brings a radical and secular perspective to
political, economic, social and cultural issues and controversies
in Jewish life and to issues affecting other minority communities
struggling against oppression.

Subscription £7.50 (UK) or £15 Sterling (overseas) from
Jewish Socialist, BM 3725, London WC1N 3XX.